kinnikinnick

the mountain flower book

by

millie miller

Johnson Publishing Company

Starflower

lithophragma parviflora
saxifrage   8-20"
  a slender inhabitant
of rich dry places

Engelman aster

aster engelmannii
  composite   2-6'
    adds a shaggy
    look to low
    wet woods

Strawberry

fragaria vesca
rose   3"
  low runner of moist
    woods & meadows
...makes tasty
    jam

Globeflower
trollius laxus
buttercup 6-20"
a friend of wet
meadows from low
valleys to timberline

Lily-of-the-valley
smilacina stellata
lily   1-2'
blooms early along
valley streams...
a favorite of elk

Marshmarigold
caltha leptosepala
buttercup   3-9"
'cowslip' is a water
lover of streambanks
at high elevations

Mariposa lily

calochortus nattallii
lily   8-12"
'sego lily'...
an early bloom of
open meadows
and woods

Nodding onion

allium cernuum
lily   6-18"
flavors dry
to moist areas
of foothills

Sand lily

leucocrinum montanum
lily   1-3"
a spring 'mayflower'
to brighten low
sandy foothills

Chickweed

cerastium arvense
pink   3-12"
   dense patches of
   'mouse ear' in
   sandy dry soil

Dryad

dryas hookeriana
rose   1-3"
    hardy ground cover
    of highest peaks

Sandwort

arenaria obtusiloba
pink   1-3"
   'sandywinks' mat
   rocky slopes
      above timberline

Syringa

philadelphus lewisii
hydrangea   shrub
this 'mock orange'
is the state flower
of Idaho

Thimbleberry

rubus parvifloras
rose   shrub
bears munch these
red raspberry
cousins

Serviceberry

amelanchier alnifolia
rose   shrub
an early fruit
used for pemmican
and pie

Chokecherry

prunus melanocarpa
rose   tall shrub
fine jelly &
wine from these
dense thickets

Pearly everlasting
anaphalis margaritacea
composite   1-3'
woolly little heads
from foothills to
timberline

Sagebrush
artemisia tridentata
composite   2-8'
smells like the herb
especially when wet
...flowers announce
the fall

Wyethia
wyethia helianthoides
composite   8-20"
white 'mules ears'
prefer low wet woods

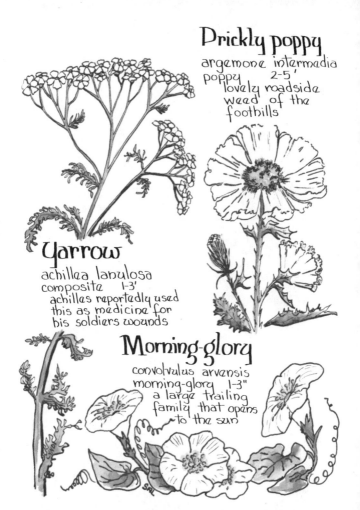

Prickly poppy
argemone intermedia
        2-5'
poppy
    lovely roadside
    weed of the
    foothills

Yarrow
achillea lanulosa
composite   1-3'
    achilles reportedly used
this as medicine for
his soldiers wounds

Morning-glory
convolvulus arvensis
morning-glory   1-3"
    a large trailing
    family that opens
    to the sun

SRL

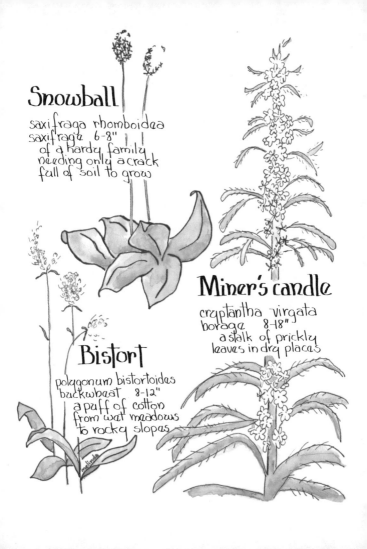

Snowball

saxifraga rhomboidea
saxifrage 6-8"
of a hardy family
needing only a crack
full of soil to grow

Miner's candle

cryptantha virgata
borage 8-18"
a stalk of prickly
leaves in dry places

Bistort

polygonum bistortoides
buckwheat 8-12"
a puff of cotton
from wet meadows
to rocky slopes

Cutleaf daisy

erigeron compositus
composite 8-12"
favors dry areas...
many daisy
relatives

Phlox

phlox multiflora
phlox 1"
often found with
'moss campion' &
'forget-me-not'

Monument plant

frasera speciosa
gentian 2-5'
'green gentian'
grows tall in
open moist areas

Evening primrose

oenothera caespitosa
evening primrose 2-4"
brightens steep sandy
places ... opens
at sunset

Bear grass

xerophyllum tenox
lily 1-2'
flowers every 5-7 years
in low woods and
meadows

Woodnymph

pyrola uniflora
wintergreen 6-8"
dainty nodder
hides by shady
streams & bogs

Yucca

yucca glauca
lily   2-4'
one specific moth
pollinates this
'spanish bayonet'

Woolly mullein

verbascum thapsus
figwort   2-8'
a velvet weed
that colonizes
disturbed areas

White clematis

clematis ligusticifolia
buttercup   up to 30'
a climbing vine that can
cover trees & bushes

Prickly pear cactus

opuntia polyacantha
cactus 4-8"
blossoms in early
spring where it's
hot and dry

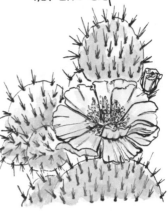

Cinquefoil

potentilla gracilis
rose 1-2'
dots low valleys
and moist
meadows

Buttercup

ranunculus glaberrimus
buttercup 6-12"
shiny blooms of
early spring

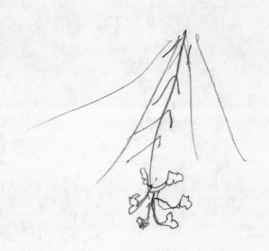

Avalanche lily

erythronium grandiflorum
lily   1-2"
        a snow flower
    west of the
    continental divide

Golden pea

thermopsis montana
pea   1-4'
        a 'golden banner'
    that announces
            spring

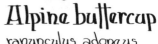

Alpine buttercup

ranunculus adoneus
buttercup   4-12"
    pushes itself up
        through the
            snow

Stonecrop
sedum stenopetalum
orpine   4-8"
   in rocky dry soil
   a waxy cover
      slows water
         loss

Rabbitbrush
chrysothamnus nauseosus
composite   2-3'
   this late bloomer
   thrives on poor soil
   where others cannot

Avens
dryas drummondii
rose   2-4"
   hardy blossom
   found on high
   gravel slopes

Dandelion

taraxacum officinale
composite   3-6"
brightens the
world all
summer long

Butter-&-eggs

linaria vulgaris
figwort   6-18"
discovered near
old mines
and cabins

Monkey flower

mimulus guttatus
figwort   2-18"
drinks from springs &
beaver dams... other
monkey colors too

Violet

viola nuttallii
violet   2-4"
    johnnys jump up
    early spring &
    in other colors

Ragwort

senecio integerrimus
composite   1-3'
'groundsel' likes lots
of space ...comes
from a large family

Sulphurflower

eriogonum umbellatum
buckwheat   4-16"
brightens dry slopes
of open low
valleys

Wallflower

erysimum capitatum
mustard   1-3'
beautiful hues
… companion
of the pines

Hollygrape

mahonia repens
barberry   1-3"
in the fall,
the leaves
turn red

Salsify

tragopogon dubius
composite   1-4'
like a big ripe
dandelion by
roads & fences

Arnica

arnica cordifolia
composite 8-24"
sheltered under
the quaking aspen

Blanketflower

gaillardia aristata
composite 8-30"
these handsome
'firewheels' bring
in the summer

Mules-ears

wyethia amplexicaulis
composite 1-2'
an early bloomer
...cousin to 'white
wyethia

Sticky gumweed

grindelia squarrosa
composite 6-30"
sticky flowers &
leaves dot fences
and roadsides

Sunflower

helianthus annuus
composite 1-8'
state flower of Kansas
often found along
roadsides

Blackeyed susan

rudbeckia hirta
composite 6-24"
enjoys dry meadows
and mountainsides

Balsamroot

balsamorhiza hookeri
composite   8-24"
blooms early in
dry valleys

Alpine sunflower

hymenoxys grandiflora
composite   8-12"
'old man of the
mountain' always
faces the rising sun

Woolly yellowdaisy

eriophyllum lanatum
composite   4-24"
very common in
dry areas of the
foothills

Springbeauty

claytonia lanceolata
purslane   6"
  this wood border
  has little potatoes
  at roots end

Lewisia

lewisia pygmaea
purslane   1-3"
  a tiny little thing
  nam'd for Lewis
  (of Lewis & Clark)

Bitterroot

lewisia radiviva
purslane   3"
  Montana's state
  flower blooms early
  & does indeed taste bitter

SALLY

Twinflower

linnaea borealis
honeysuckle   3"
   dainty sisters hidden
   low in wet and
   shady places

Rosecrown

sedum rhodanthum
orpine   6-12"
   'queen's crown' reigns
   in the rocky nooks
   of streambanks

Moss campion

silene acaulis
pink   1"
   mossy cushions
   sharing hi elevations
   with phlox &
   forget-me-nots

Wild rose

rosa woodsii
rose   a shrub
  prickly thickets
    along open
      streambanks

Milkweed

asclepias speciosa
milkweed   2-4'
  a fragrant plant
  with milky juice
  in stem & leaves

Mountain heath

phyllodoce empetriformis
    heath   8-20"
  an evergreen shrub
  found in wet places
often mats rocks

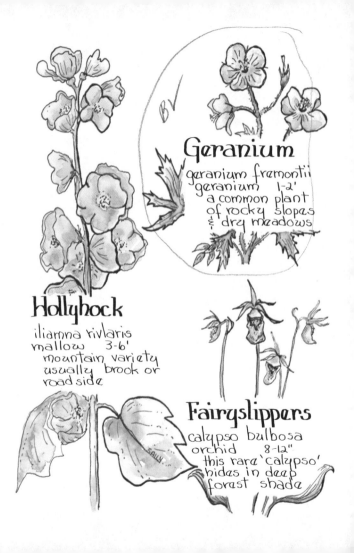

Geranium

geranium fremontii
geranium 1-2'
a common plant
of rocky slopes
& dry meadows

Hollyhock

iliamna rivlaris
mallow   3-6'
mountain variety
usually brook or
road side

Fairyslippers

calypso bulbosa
orchid   8-12"
this rare 'calypso'
hides in deep
forest shade

Red elephant

pedicularis groenlandica
figwort   8-24"
    clumps through
    bogs & meadows
    of open spaces

Horsemint

monarda menthaefolia
mint   1-3'
    a tasty tea
    of foothill valleys

Bush
penstemon

penstemon fruticosus
figwort   6-20"
    low thick patches
    in dry places...
    many relatives

Fireweed

epilobium angustifolium
evening primrose 1-7'
   sympathetic to fire
   scarred areas...
   a favorite of bears

Fleabane

erigeron speciosus
composite   6-30"
   abundant late
   summer in moist
   shady places

Jacobs-ladder

polemonium pulchellum
phlox   1-12"
   seeks protection in
   rocky crevices...
   of a large family

Aster

aster integrifolius
composite   1-2'
a fall family
residing mostly
in open woods

Locoweed

oxytropis lambertii
pea   8-10"
related to pea & vetch
but this one drives
horses plum 'loco'

Townsendia

townsendia sericea
composite   1-12"
single flower atop
a short stem
in dry areas

Bristle thistle

carduus nutans
composite   2-3'
insects drawn to
the rich nectar of
this roadside plant

Bull thistle

cirsium vulgare
composite   2-5'
full of thistle-down
to tinder your
campfire

Beeplant

cleome serrulata
caper   2-5'
bees attracted to
this 'stinkweed'
of sandy places

Primrose

primula parryi
primrose 6-18"
   a sturdy bloom
    by high
    mountain
     streams

Shooting star

dodacatheon paucifloram
primrose   6-16"
  shines in wet open
  places from lowest
  valleys to highest peaks

Mountain-sorrel

oxyria digyna
buckwheat 6-12"
  prefers shady wet
  places on rocky
  slopes & ledges

Indian paintbrush

castilleja integra
figwort 8-12"
many colors &
varieties

Kinnikinnick

arctostaphylos uva-ursi
heath   1-3"
   a ground cover
   known as 'bearberry'
found in woods & sand
from sea to mountain tops

Wintergreen

gaultheria humifusa
heath   1-3"
a creeping evergreen
with a wintergreen
   flavor

SALLY

Wood lily
lilium umbellatum
lily
15"
brightens shady
stream banks

Scarlet gilia
gilia aggregata
phlox
18"
trumpets in dry
patches from
foothills to
timberline

Anemone
anemone globosa
buttercup
12"
a secret of high
shady valleys

Forget-me-not

myosotis alpestris
borage 4-12"
slender delicate
hue of high
meadows

Penstemon

penstemon cyaneus
figwort 6-20"
the 'beard-tongue'
has many kin of
varied colors

Alpine
Forget-me-not

eritrichium elongatum
borage 2-4"
a fragrant
cushion of the
mountain-tops

Wild hyacinth
brodiaea douglasii
lily   1-3'
nods in dry
rocky places
& open woods

Harebell
campanula rotundifolia
bluebell   8-20"
this Blueball of
Scotland rings late
into the fall

Chiming bells
mertensia ciliata
borage   1-2'
leafy bed for elk
young & winter stash
for rock rabbit

Columbine

aquilegia coarulea
buttercup 8-24"
graceful state flower
   of Colorado...
also red & yellow

Sky pilot

polemonium viscosum
phlox   12"
   said to smell like
'skunkweed' when
walked upon

Blue-eyed grass

sisyrinchium sarmentosum
iris   5-12"
   delicate & grassy...
in open wet areas
   of low valleys

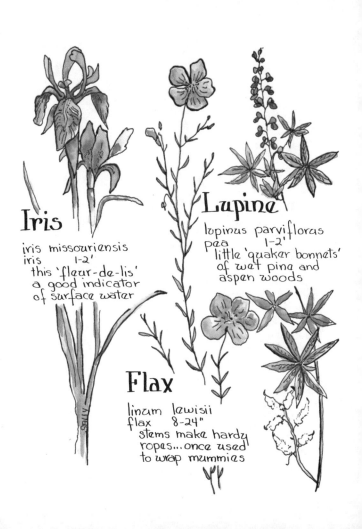

Iris

iris missouriensis
iris   1-2'
  this 'fleur-de-lis'
  a good indicator
  of surface water

Lupine

lupinus parvifloras
pea   1-2'
  little 'quaker bonnets'
  of wet pine and
  aspen woods

Flax

linum   lewisii
flax   8-24"
  stems make hardy
  ropes...once used
  to wrap mummies

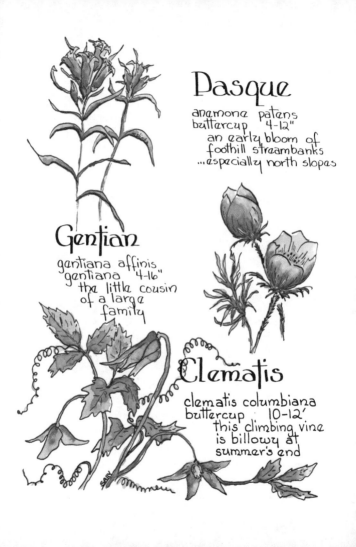

Pasque

anemone patens
buttercup   4-12"
an early bloom of
foothill streambanks
...especially north slopes

Gentian

gentiana affinis
gentiana   4-16"
the little cousin
of a large
family

Clematis

clematis columbiana
buttercup   10-12'
this climbing vine
is billowy at
summer's end

Larkspur

delphinium nelsoni
buttercup   6-24"
  abundant in sage...
  deadly to cattle
  but not to sheep

Monkshood

aconitum columbianum
buttercup   2-5'
  cloisters by wet
  meadows and
  streams

Vetch

vicia americana
pea   1-4'
  a climbing vine
  of moist
  open woods

Mountain gentian

gentiana calycosa
gentian 4-16"
graces wet
  meadows of
  high rockies

Camas

camassia quamash
lily   1-2'
indians & settlers
used these bulbs
  as potatoes

Purple fringe

phacelia sericea
waterleaf   5-18"
boarders high
  mountain trails
  roadsides

flowers drawn by...

Melinda Lucas

CINDY NELSON

SALLY KING

Dedication...

to **Minka**
my ol' puppy &
trail companion

references...

Clements, Frederic E.
and Edith S.. <u>Rocky
Mountain Flowers</u>.
New York: The H.W.
Wilson Co., 1945.

Craighead, John J,
Frank C. Craighead and
Ray J. Davis. <u>A Field
Guide to Rocky Mountain
Wildflowers</u>. Boston:
Houghton Mifflin Co., 1963.

Nelson, Ruth
Ashton. <u>Plants of
Rocky Mountain
National Park</u>. Rocky
Mountain Nature
Association, Inc., 1976.

Roberts, Harold &
Rhoda. <u>Colorado
Wild Flowers</u>. Denver:
Bradford-Robinson
Printing Co., 1967.

Weber, William A..
<u>Rocky Mountain Flora</u>.
Boulder: Colorado
Associated University
Press, 1972.